Balloon Stickers
Dinosaur
Island ACTIVITY
BOOK

make
believe
ideas

Balloon Stickers
Dinosaur Island ACTIVITY BOOK

Dare to enter this prehistoric paradise
and meet some fearsome friends along the way!

•

Color, doodle, and puzzle your way through the
amazing activities. Then press out and create
characters, games, masks, a poster, and more!

•

You can use your balloon stickers in the book, to finish
your press-out pieces, or anywhere else you want!

How to use your
PRESS-OUT PIECES:

At the back of the book, there are fun press-outs for you to make, create, and play with.

1 Pull out the card pages at the back of the book.

MIGHTY MASK
Press out the mask, eye holes, and small holes either side. Then thread some ribbon through the holes and tie it around your head to finish!

BRILLIANT BANNER
Press out the shapes. Then thread some ribbon through the holes to create a brilliant banner. Hang it wherever you want!

2 Gently push the shapes until they pop out.

DINO QUIZ

Put the dinosaurs in height order from the smallest to the tallest. Write the letters in the spaces below.

A

B

C

D

smallest **B** .... **C** .... **A** .... **D** .... tallest

Find and circle three orange creatures.

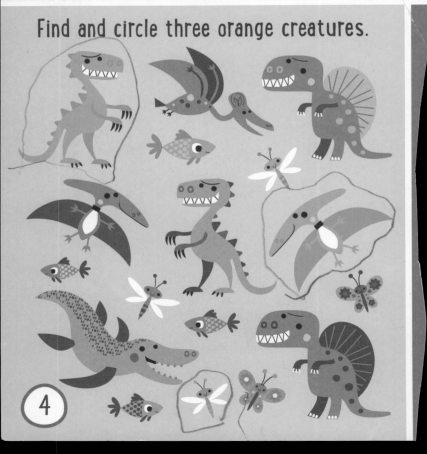

Which one doesn't belong?

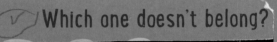

4

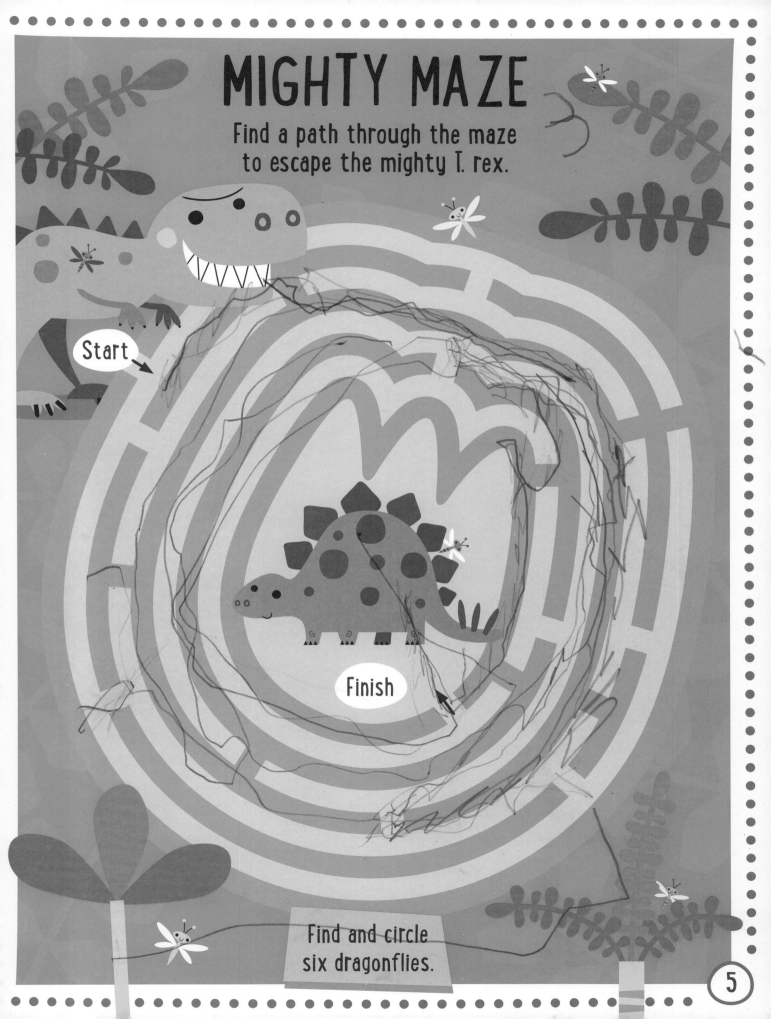

SNOWY SCENE

Guide Parasaurolophus Penny down the ski slope.
Try to do it without touching the sides!

Start →

Finish ←

Who doesn't belong
in this scene?

Can you find the dinosaur
with this silhouette?

Trace the snowball trails.

7

DINOSAUR DIG

Can you find all of the dinosaur patterns in the grid?
Check the boxes when you find them.

FISHING FABROSAURUS

Follow the lines to see which
Fabrosaurus has caught a boot.

Which dinosaur has
caught the most fish?
Write the letter. (.........)

DINO DETECTIVE

Use the clues to find out who took T. rex Ted's tasty ham.

Clue 1:
The dinosaur has green spots.

Clue 2:
The dinosaur has orange claws.

Clue 3:
The dinosaur has a blue frill.

Parasaurolophus Pippa

Diplodocus Dan

Spinosaurus Sid

Lambeosaurus Lil

Stegosaurus Sam

Allosaurus Ann

Which dinosaur stole T. rex Ted's ham?

....

10

DISCO DANCERS

Color the disco scene.
Use the dots to guide you.

VOLCANO VIEW

The dinosaurs are playing hide-and-seek.

Search the scene for the things below.
Check the boxes when you find them.

1 Stegosaurus

2 fish

2 Triceratops

4 bones

3 Brachiosaurus

5 eggs

SWEET SWEATERS

Design cool sweaters for the dinosaurs.

YOU CRACK ME UP

Find the eggs that look exactly like these.

Draw a baby dino. Use the grid to guide you.

DINOSAUR ISLAND

Solve the riddle, and then circle where
you think Diplodocus Daisy should live.

RIDDLE

Within my trees all creatures roam.
You should choose me for your home.

VOLCANO
VIEW

JURASSIC
JUNGLE

COOL COVE

Now use the symbol chart to break the code and find the answer:

J _ R _ _ _ _ _

N _ _ _ _ E

MOUNT MIGHTY

SCARY SWAMP

DARING DESERT

A = ▲
B = ★
C = ✺
D = ♛
E = ▶
F = 🌰
G = 🦋
H = 🍃
I = ◀
J = ✳
K = ❀
L = 🌰
M = 🍃
N = ✿
O = ●
P = ✕
Q = ★
R = ◉
S = ✶
T = ✳
U = 🌷
V = ▼
W = 🥚
X = ✚
Y = ✺
Z = 🥚

SWIM-A-THON

Find the route to the finish line. Use the key below.

Can you find eight
red starfish?

Color the volcano.

Join the dots to
reveal who is hiding.

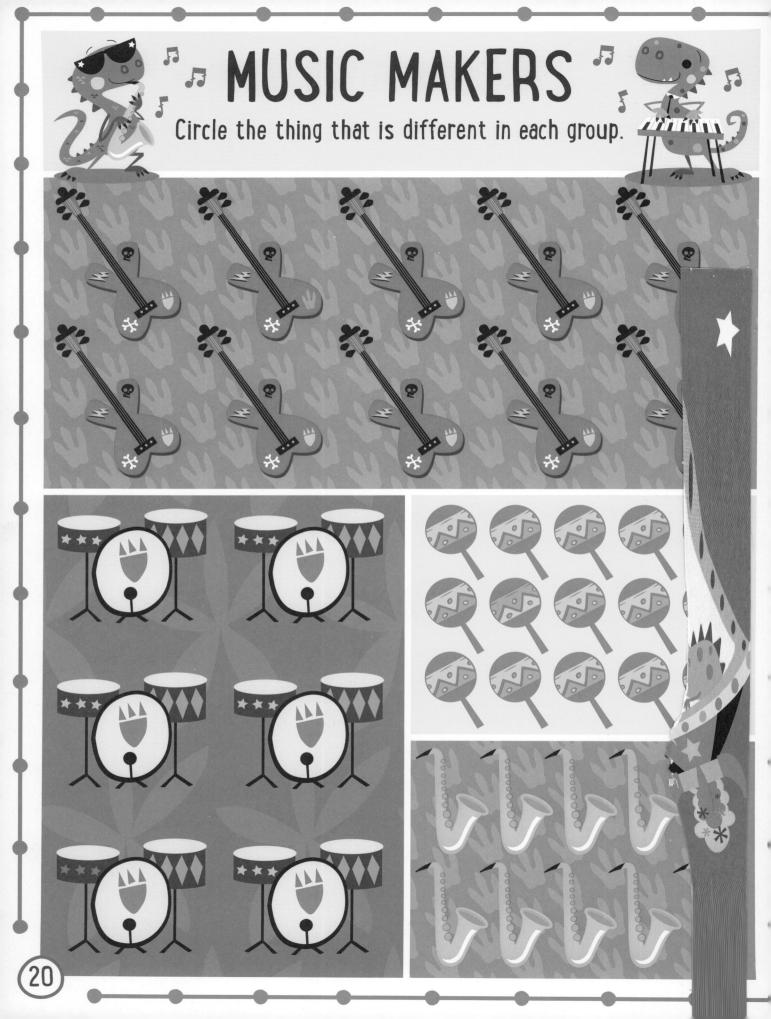

MUSIC MAKERS

Circle the thing that is different in each group.

FOSSIL FINDS

Find all six words in the grid. Words can go down or across.

bone   dig   extinct

fossil   rock   skull

```
a n c f o s s i l l
c l p d r d i g e b
r b d k e x f t i m
e o i j x t n w k u
h n g q t a c s s k
l e n e i c k i k g
i n e s n x t v u z
f g r o c k c r l b
g y a m t i f x l a
o c t o s b n o e w
```

Find and circle four fireflies.

25

WATER SPORTS

Color the scene.

Search the scene for the things below.
Check the boxes when you find them.

26

1 kayak

2 Jet Skis

1 speedboat

helmets

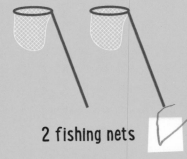

2 fishing nets

2 life buoys

DINOSAUR DATES

Draw lines to match each dinosaur to its perfect partner.

Look at the pictures to answer the sums.
Circle each dinosaur's perfect match.

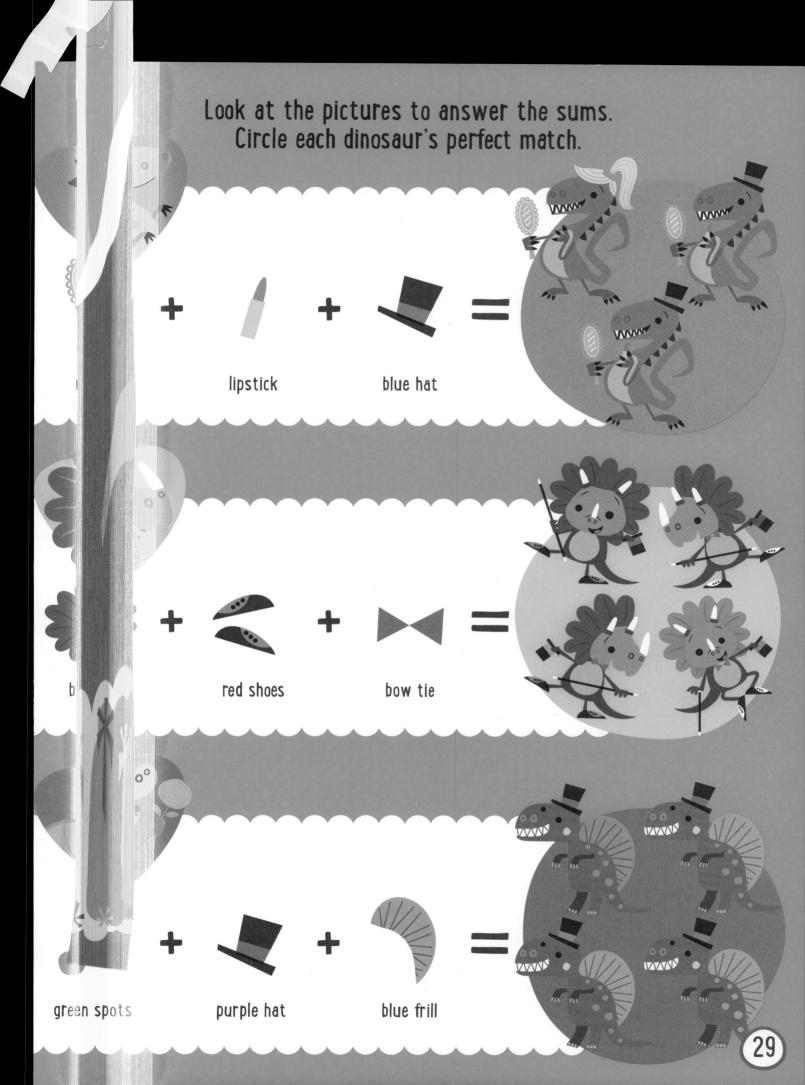

+ lipstick + blue hat =

+ red shoes + bow tie =

green spots + purple hat + blue frill =

CIRCUS SEQUENCE

Use color to finish the patterns.

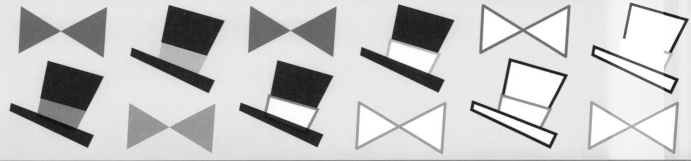

DINO DOODLES

Copy and color the dinos.
Use the grids to guide you.

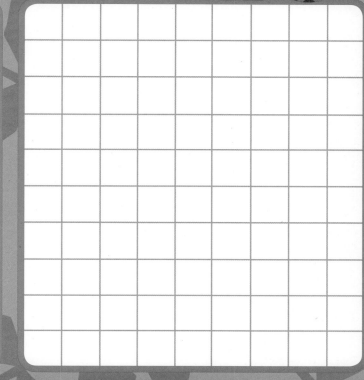

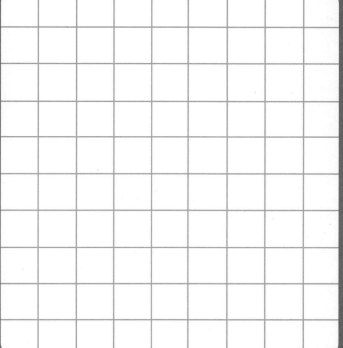

STAR SWEEP

Find the path back to the nest. Collect all the stars along the way.

Start →

Finish

How many stars
did you collect?
Write the answer.

JURASSIC JUMBLE

Unscramble the words below. Use the pictures to guide you.

b e o n ....

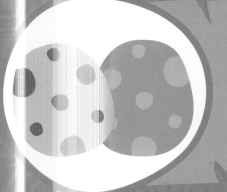 .... g e s g

e a c v ....

 .... i o n d

ROARSOME ROYALTY

Join the dots to finish the castle. Then color it in.

Find and circle
seven jewels.

Use doodles and color to design a crown for King Velociraptor.

Trace the lines to finish the tea set.

35

FLIGHT ACADEMY

Trace the words to reveal what each dinosaur is flying.

balloon

glider

rocket

Find and circle the dinosaur that looks like this.

ON THE RED CARPET

Find and circle eight differences between the scenes.

SNACK ATTACK

Count the snacks to finish the sums.

$$2 + 2 = 4$$

$$2 + 3 = 5$$

$$5 + 3 = 8$$

$$4 + 6 = 10$$

WHERE AM I?

Circle the pictures to answer the questions.

Who is wearing a hat? **Who is singing?** **Who is looking in the mirror?**

Who is playing the keyboard? Who is wearing a bow tie?

COOL QUAD BIKES

Find a path through the racetrack to the finish flag.

Start

Finish